PRACTICAL

DAIL

By the same author
APPLIED MAGIC
ASPECTS OF OCCULTISM
THE COSMIC DOCTRINE
ESOTERIC PHILOSOPHY OF LOVE AND MARRIAGE
PSYCHIC SELF-DEFENCE
SANE OCCULTISM
THE TRAINING AND WORK OF AN INITIATE
THROUGH THE GATES OF DEATH

Occult Fiction
THE DEMON LOVER

PRACTICAL OCCULTISM IN DAILY LIFE

by
DION FORTUNE

THE AQUARIAN PRESS
Wellingborough, Northamptonshire

First published 1935
Sixth Impression 1971
First paperback Edition 1976
Second Impression 1978

© THE SOCIETY OF THE INNER LIGHT 1976

This book is sold subject to the condition that it shall not, by way of trade or otherwise, be lent, re-sold, hired out, or otherwise circulated without the publisher's prior consent in any form of binding or cover other than that in which it is published and without a similar condition, including this condition, being imposed on the subsequent purchaser.

ISBN 0 85030 133 5 (UK)
ISBN 0 87728 316 8 (USA)

Printed and bound in Great Britain by
Weatherby Woolnough, Wellingborough
Northamptonshire

CONTENTS

CHAPTER
- I. PRACTICAL OCCULTISM IN DAILY LIFE *page* 7
- II. PRACTICAL OCCULTISM IN DAILY LIFE—*continued* 13
- III. THE CONTROL OF ENVIRONMENT 17
- IV. REMEMBERING PAST INCARNATIONS 22
- V. REMEMBERING PAST INCARNATIONS—*continued* 26
- VI. WORKING OUT KARMA 30
- VII. WORKING OUT KARMA—*continued* 35
- VIII. DIVINATION : ITS USES AND LIMITS 39
- IX. THE USE AND ABUSE OF MIND POWER 43
- X. ETHERIC MAGNETISM 50
- XI. ETHERIC MAGNETISM—*continued* 55
- XII. THE PROBLEM OF THE UNPOLARIZED 61

CHAPTER I

PRACTICAL OCCULTISM IN DAILY LIFE

A LARGE number of letters pass through the office of the Society of the Inner Light, and a considerable proportion of these letters ask for help and advice concerning the application of occult forces and methods to the problems of everyday life. Obsessions, hauntings, occult attacks are comparatively rare and, as often as not, when investigated, turn out to be insane delusions. But persistent runs of bad luck; ill health which does not yield to ordinary methods of treatment, and concerning which doctors either disagree or declare they can find nothing the matter; disturbances due to unsound methods of psychic development, and evil influences in houses and places—these form a constant feature of our correspondence. We are also frequently asked concerning the interpretation of dream and vision symbols and the recovery of memories of past incarnations.

According to orthodox occult tradition the Mystery teaching should be strictly reserved for those who have offered the unreserved dedication and have had years of training and passed exacting tests. In other words, occultism meant adepthood or nothing. But with the general spread of occult knowledge which is taking place at the present time, a change is coming over the spirit of the movement. Just as community singing has taught everyone to enjoy taking part in the rendering of music, so the wayfaring man is asking that he shall be enabled to apply the methods of which he reads to the problems of his daily life. One cannot deny that this is a very reasonable request.

It is a difficult problem, however, to know how far the metaphysical and meta-psychic theories and methods of occultism can be made available for the untrained person, who is very apt to get hold of things by the wrong end and so enmesh himself still worse in his difficulties. A special attitude and viewpoint is necessary for the satisfactory operation of occult forces; the man who would use them must be free from emotional bias and entirely detached and serene in his attitude, otherwise he makes confusion worse confounded. A knowledge of technicalities is not enough for occult work; it is the attitude that is all-important and that determines the nature of the ultimate issue. This attitude can only be arrived at by self-discipline and purification of character.

It is possible, however, to explain quite simply and practically what the requirements are, to teach the occult doctrines in their entirety, as this Society has long been doing, and to explain enough of methods of a suitable type to enable any reasonably intelligent and well-balanced person to make practical use of them in the everyday problems of life, even if its major ills must still be left to the expert.

The greater ceremonial methods are, of course, unsuitable for the use of anyone save a trained initiate; but there are many minor rites that can be used by anyone who can achieve a steady concentration. Moreover, an understanding of the occult principles applying to every-day life is invaluable as a prophylactic, enabling us to save ourselves from all manner of troubles. It also shows us the best way in which to approach and handle our problems, for there is a strategic approach to every problem—the flanking attack that out-manœuvres, instead of the frontal attack of blind force. There are also tides in the affairs of men, and we may just as well time our operations so that we have these tides with us instead of against us. All these things are practical applications of occultism to everyday life, a knowledge of which must be of benefit.

So far as is possible, then, I propose to teach these things, and to teach them, not as rule-of-thumb methods, but with explanations of the occult principles on which they rest, so that those who try to use them may use them intelligently. How far they succeed depends upon the judgment they use in discerning the nature of the problems with which they are confronted. Diagnosis must always precede treatment, and the diagnosis of subtle psychic conditions is by no means a simple matter, because the subconscious element has to be recognised and allowed for, and it is not easy to be sufficiently impersonal and unbiassed to achieve this when our problems are pressing acutely. However, we can but do the best we know, and we can often succeed in being more honest with ourselves than we are when we are trying to justify our position in the eyes of another.

Success also depends on our power to concentrate, holding the mind steady on a single idea. This, however, is almost entirely a matter of practice, and the regular use of certain exercises usually develops the required capacity fairly quickly.

Given these two things—a right judgment as to the nature of the problem and ability to concentrate, a great deal can be done, even by the uninitiated and untrained. Some problems can be worked out in their entirety and all problems can be made easier to bear, even if they remain unsolved.

It must not be thought, however, that I am going to teach how to blow the trumpets of Jericho. Some problems, of course, clear up readily when the underlying psychic cause is dealt with; others require steady and long-continued work for their solving. In others again, a mistaken diagnosis renders the work abortive. The experienced occultist, dealing with matters on the spot, ought to be able to make his diagnosis and forecast the outlook with a high degree of accuracy; but I am not writing for experienced occultists, but for those who are spelling out the letters of the occult alphabet; and although I am always glad to advise, as far as lies in my power, on such matters, it is seldom possible for me to be on the spot. The reader of these pages, therefore, will have to learn his lessons with the help of experience, which is an expensive school, but a very efficient one.

BASIC PRINCIPLES

There are many old-fashioned books, and some newer ones, too, which call themselves "Home Doctors" or some such name. They tabulate a list in symptoms such as Stomach ; pain in ; sensation of fullness in, etc., and give a reference to the page where the appropriate remedy is listed, usually in doses suitable for navvies and blacksmiths. These are singularly unsatisfactory compilations, and probably send up the death-rate considerably by virtue of delayed operations and unrecognized cancer.

I do not propose to make that mistake in these pages, but to ask of the reader sufficient effort and attention to grasp certain basic principles in order that he may first and foremost arrive at a diagnosis and apply the occult methods intelligently.

First of all, we have to realize that the material plane, as we see it, is the end-result of a long chain of evolutionary processes that have gone on in the subtler planes, the realms of spirit, mind, and astral ether. Consequently, every problem that we meet with on the physical plane will have a kind of soul, as it were, composed of factors from each of these levels of manifestation. It is important for us to realize this, because every problem is composite, and we have to determine the relative proportion of these different factors and discern upon which level the trouble has its root or nucleus. It is no use trying to deal with a problem by a simple astral exorcism if its root lies in some spiritual factor deep hidden in the soul.

We must always remember, however, that each plane has its own laws and conditions, and that these cannot be overridden by any power, however great, but only directed and used. But because each plane is ensouled and directed by the plane above, the extent to which its forces and mechanisms can be modified and directed is very great—much greater than is generally suspected. Nevertheless, there are well-defined limits to this power, and these must be accepted. It is in this respect that spiritual healing so often comes to grief, for it seldom admits limitations to what it is pleased to call the power of God, but which in all too many cases means the desire of the sufferer to be relieved from discomfort.

We must next realize that there are many forces, and many forms of existence, which do not extend down the planes as far as the physical; they may possess, for instance, a spiritual and mental, or spiritual, mental, and astro-etheric aspect, but no physical form. If we know how, we can in many cases extend these forces down the planes, and give them expression on the physical plane. This does not mean, however, that we are going to effect miracles and materializations, for in the great majority of cases the chosen vehicle of manifestation is the mind of the operator, and the operation therefore appears to take place by a concurrence of lucky chances in the way of nature. It is the power systematically, in chosen cases, to command these "lucky chances," which shows that definite operations are being performed.

It must be noted, however, that discrimination has to be used in choosing suitable cases for these methods; they cannot be used as a routine operation for all who are uncomfortable in mind, body, or estate, and desire alterations.

It is the cases wherein these subtle forces are the predominant factors that are suitable for occult operations, and yield to them in a remarkably dramatic manner. But in all cases, however apparently materialistic, these subtle forces play a part, and they can be used to alleviate, if not to cure. A man crushed in a railway accident, for instance, or in the grip of an acute infection such as pneumonia, appears to have all his problems on the physical plane; yet this is far from being the case, for surgical shock and resistance to infection play a very important part in the issue, and these things belong to the subtler planes, for they depend upon vitality and temperament.

We must also remember that in order to assess with accuracy the nature of many types of problem, especially those relating to runs of bad luck and psychic pathologies, we must take into account the karma, or influences of previous incarnations. There are certain methods of assessing these, which we will describe in due course. Moreover, individual karma, or destiny, has to be worked out under the influence of the larger cycle of racial karma, which modifies or reinforces it, and this must also be taken into account.

To sum up, then, every problem is fourfold, spiritual, mental, astro-etheric, and physical. Each of these planes has its own laws, which cannot be abrogated, but can be directed. The causation of most problems also extends backwards in time to previous incarnations, and they are modified in their working out by the prevailing influences of racial karma. It is in relation to all these factors, and not just one of them, that we have to work out our problems, and the proportions in which they are present vary in every problem.

CHAPTER II

PRACTICAL OCCULTISM IN DAILY LIFE

—continued

THERE are faculties in the soul of man which correspond to the subtler planes of existence, which exert an influence on these planes, and are in turn influenced by them. Most people ignore the existence of these planes and these faculties; yet if we observe life as it goes past us, we cannot fail to be struck by the fact that there are tides and eddies in the affairs of men which cannot be explained by the material sequence of cause and effect. It is these subtle tides and eddies that the occultist studies, and he has been able as a result of his studies to formulate certain definite laws with regard to them; these laws have a very immediate application to daily life and its problems.

These different planes do not lie one above another like the strata of rocks; they are different modes of existence, and can, any and all of them, occupy the same space at the same time, as sound, light, and warmth may do. The different aspects of consciousness are built up out of these different modes of existence just as the calcium which forms our bones is drawn from the mineral kingdom of the earth, and the water in our tissues is derived from the springs and rivers.

The calcium in our bones is in no way different from the calcium to be found in the tissues of plants or in the rocks of the earth's surface. Calcium behaves in the same way, and obeys the same laws wherever it is found; and so does water. Our heart is a pump just like any other pump, and the water in our blood behaves no differently to the water in the hot-water pipes. Precisely the same conditions prevail in the sphere of consciousness. The spark of Divine Spirit, which is the innermost core and nucleus of every human soul, is part of the Kingdom of

Heaven. Our mental powers with their forces and images are part of the kingdom of mind; our emotional and instinctive nature is part of what occultists call the astral kingdom; and our body in its subtle etheric and dense physical aspect forms part of the kingdom of earth, though be it remembered that earth has a subtle electro-magnetic aspect as well as a dense one.

Our body receives impressions from the physical plane through the five physical senses. It cannot perceive thought, or emotion, or the things of the spirit, save in so far as they are signalled to it by the effect they have on someone's body. But there are subtle senses, rudimentary in most people, more highly developed in some, which correspond to the three subtle levels of existence.

Most of us know instinctively the emotional state of anyone with whom we are in close touch; we know whether he is displeased, depressed, or frightened, even though he show no outward sign of his condition and may do his best to conceal it. The horse knows when the rider is afraid; the newborn child knows the difference between the nurse who will control it effectually and the mother who will give in to it, and behaves accordingly.

To explain these things as the subconscious interpretation of subtleties of gesture and expression makes demands on our credulity which are quite unnecessary. A far simpler and more comprehensive hypothesis explains that these things are due to the direct perception of emotional states by the corresponding factor in our consciousness, which reacts to them. Observe how the depressed person depresses his companions; how the angry one irritates them; how the timid one invites aggression.

We are influenced far more than we realize by the mental states of those about us; it is for this reason that a good morale is all-important in any organization. The bad employer does not realize this, and thinks that sullen and resentful workpeople can give him just as good value for the wages he pays as loyal and cheerful ones. One person in a workshop with a sense of injury will demoralize all the rest of the employees, even if he, for reasons of his own, gives no open expression to his grievance. If we observe business houses we shall see how the mental attitude of the person at the head goes right down through the whole staff, including those who have no personal contact with him. The inharmonious person works up resistances all round him which make life very heavy going for him. A kindly, genial, and even-tempered attitude is an effectual lubricant which by reducing friction increases power.

Does it follow from this that we are to yield ourselves without effort to the influences of whatever atmosphere we may find ourselves in? We are unwise if we do. Even if the atmosphere is congenial, it is not well to become too dependent on it lest we make ourselves so sensitive that we succumb to the least roughness when we have to face the outside world. If the atmosphere is uncongenial we need definite mental armour to protect us from its influences. Some teachers would say that we ought to set to work and reform the whole condition by means of thought power. Many novels have been written, and plays too, such as *The Passing of the Third Floor Back*, in support of this thesis, but this is an ambitious goal to set before ourselves at the start, and we may be wiser to content ourselves with the control of the inner kingdom to begin with. In any case, we cannot exercise much influence on our environment until it has ceased to have influence over us.

But while we need to recognize the very potent effect that a mental atmosphere can have upon us, let us remember that atmospheres are things which are made by human minds, and that we need not, and should not, yield ourselves inert and unresisting to their influence, but can do something towards the making of atmospheres on our own account. If we find ourselves in an atmosphere of disruption and discontent, we can set to work and make a centre of serenity and steadfastness in our own immediate neighbourhood. This we do by working from within outward, and by controlling our own reactions to the inharmonious environment.

As soon as the mental atmosphere ceases to be able to affect us, we are beginning to affect it. The stabilized inner atmosphere overflows, and the circle of harmony spreads like the ripples in a pool. Soon the more sensitive among our neighbours begin to feel the new influence that has been introduced into the mental atmosphere; they react to it in their turn and the influence is reinforced.

If, however, we had set to work in the first place to alter conditions which caused us unhappiness in order to recover our peace of mind, we should have failed to attain our end; for however much we might make and remake the world nearer to our heart's desire, there would still be the crumpled rose-leaf such as disturbed the princess in the fairy tale. But if we obtain dominion over the Inner Kingdom and are able to hold it steady in the face of external influences, so that we can say with St. Paul, "None of these things move me, . . ." we have become a factor to be reckoned with in the mental atmosphere; ceasing to be influenced, we become an influence.

There is an old story of two travellers who found the road rough to their feet. One said, "Let us kill all the cattle in the world, and tan their hides, and make a carpet to cover the road from end to end so that we may walk in comfort." But the other said, "That is not possible, for the road is longer than the skins of all the cows in the country. Let us out of a single hide make shoes for our feet, and then our smooth carpet will go with us wherever we tread."

The man who wants to alter his environment until he is happy is like the traveller who wanted to carpet the entire road; but the man who has gained control of his own reactions and rules his Inner Kingdom is like the man who has made shoes to protect his feet from the roughness of the path.

We must realize two things, then, if we are to avail ourselves of the Ancient Wisdom. Firstly, mental and emotional conditions have power to affect us without overt physical action; secondly, we must not allow reactions to these influences to gallop about like wild horses, but must break them in to harness. To perceive an influence is not necessarily to react to it. There is such a thing as counteracting it, and it is this which occult knowledge can teach us to do.

CHAPTER III

THE CONTROL OF ENVIRONMENT

AS we saw in the previous chapter, the control of environment must begin with self-control, and until we cease to be influenced by surrounding conditions we cannot hope to exercise any mental influence over them. Paradoxically, it is only when our environment ceases to matter to us that we have the power to change it by mental means.

Having reached the point when we can obtain inner harmony, even if it be only for brief periods, we are in a position to undertake practical mental work; let us then consider how to set about this all-important task. Meditation should always precede any action or decision, and the meditation should be, curiously enough, not upon the subject of the problem that is to be solved, but rather upon spiritual development and unfoidment; upon selfless dedication to the highest ideal that can be conceived, and upon a clear and concrete formulation of that ideal itself. Then we should rise still higher in our aspiration, and meditate upon the limitless outpouring of spiritual life from which our individual lives take their rise, and should say over and over to ourselves as a mantram or litany the words, "Limitless power. Absolute harmony. Eternal duration," imaging the Absolute as white radiance pouring down upon us and our environment as we do so. We should live our lives and do our work to the accompaniment of this refrain for days together, until we find that it is beginning to take hold of us and repeat itself as a tune does that runs in one's head.

When this occurs and we find that the mantram is repeating itself automatically, we know that it has gone down into the subconscious mind and is reappearing on the surface again. Now we are in a position to do practical mental work because we have made subconscious contact with the Infinite, and even before any mental work is planned or done we shall be conscious of an inner change, a sense of wider life, of power, and freedom. The effect of these rhythmic repetitions of significant phrases is very great, as Coué showed in his system of auto-suggestion and as the Catholic Church has always known and taught in the repetition of prayers upon the beads of the rosary.

As soon as this inner change begins to make itself felt we are in a position to deal magically with our environment, but not before. It is not necessary that we should have achieved a condition of permanent equilibrium, for we can hardly expect this as long as we are in incarnation; but it does mean that we shall have moments of exaltation when we have risen above our environment and can say with St. Paul—"None of these things move me."

Diagnosis, however, must always precede treatment; and before we can decide what remedy is needed we must classify the conditions with which we have to deal. This classification should always begin with our own subjective conditions, and we should ask ourselves what weaknesses in our nature have laid us open to the conditions of which we complain; and we shall find that lack of judgment, lack of endurance, lack of courage, lack of foresight, lack of energy, and many more of the little foxes that spoil the vines have been at the bottom of the trouble. Looking back over our lives we shall see many things that we should have done otherwise if we had been wiser and stronger. At this stage of the process we must never allow ourselves to lay the responsibility at the door of any other person or circumstance. If we have been wrongly dealt with by some person, we should not hold that person responsible and ourselves blameless, but should condemn ourselves for having been foolish enough to trust them, or having lacked the courage to resist them.

Having diagnosed our own weaknesses, our next task is to meditate upon the compensating qualities of those weaknesses. It is easy enough to find the opposite of the moral qualities that shall compensate any defect or overplus, but many people wonder how they can compensate for lack of wisdom or discernment. We shall find, however, that if we meditate upon humility, upon honesty with ourselves, and the courageous facing of unpleasant facts, that wisdom and discernment will not be far to seek in the practical affairs of life.

Our next task is to bring ourselves to accept the conditions in which we find ourselves as the result of our karma, and to stop resenting them and feeling sorry for ourselves; for these conditions are the very things we need to teach us the lessons of spiritual development; therefore we should accept them as just, and seek to learn what they have to teach us in the way of experience and spiritual development. This is an all-important step, and once we have achieved it and killed self-pity and resentment against fate, we have broken the karmic bonds that bind us to our conditions, and are in a position to work off the karma by means of conscious mental action, as the adepts do. But we can never hope to escape from a condition until we have broken by means of realization the karmic bond that binds us to that condition and fulfilled its lessons. That is why talismans made by any person except the one who uses them are valueless, and why the operations of ceremonial magic directed to mundane ends are apt to induce drastic reactions. The initiated adept, when he uses magical methods, diagnoses the karmic condition first and works accordingly; but the dabbler in occultism, and especially the unfortunate who purchases talismans and suchlike from the occult wholesalers who advertise their wares, is patching at effects and leaving causes untouched;

and the cause is often at a spot remote from the effect, and sometimes responds in an unexpected manner when ignorantly tampered with. Anyone, however, who tries to work out his problems by reducing them to terms of spiritual first principles is on the right track, and has come into line with those forces which occultists call the Lords of Karma, so that these co-operate with him; and when this happens, problems clear up in a very surprising fashion.

Each of the operations described above will take several days to do; they are not things which are accomplished one after another at a single sitting. Each should be persevered with until an inner change and response is felt, and then, and then only, should the next phase be embarked upon.

Having made our peace, as it were, with the Lords of Karma, we are now in a position to turn from within outwards and contemplate our environment. When we do this we shall see that there are certain conditions which, unless we can alter them magically, must be accepted, for what cannot be cured must be endured; and also certain other conditions which, by the exercise of courage, determination, and energy, are capable of modification.

Let us consider first those conditions which we must accept as inevitable save as they are capable of magical alteration; and leaving all magical considerations for the present, make up our minds to achieve such a degree of self-control and mind training that we are able completely to prevent any emotional reaction to them, for this is the essential preliminary to magical control. We must rise above irritation by meditation on compassion and serenity; above fear and nervousness by learning to control our imagination, for fear is entirely the product of the imagination—we do not feel fear of the thing from which we are actually suffering in the immediate present—and when we remember how much we have suffered from our fears of things that never happened, and how our severest suffering has often come from things we did not anticipate, and of which therefore we felt no fear, we shall see that, although fear has its importance as a warning mechanism, it can readily overreach itself and be nothing but an intolerable nuisance, like any other bad habit, and as such is to be overcome. We should therefore train the imagination not to dwell upon things we fear, but rather to picture a happy issue out of all our afflictions and ourselves as sailing triumphantly into the port of our desires. This happy day-dreaming plays a far more important part in the lives of successful men and women than is generally realized. It is safe to say that no one who habitually indulges in timid and gloomy imaginings has ever achieved an ambitious goal. The person who habitually indulges in happy day-dreams develops a peculiar mental atmosphere which is best described by the word glamorous, and the more sensitive of the persons with whom he comes in contact are influenced by it and see him, not as he actually is, but as he pictures himself in his day-dreams. It is thus that wild-cat financiers raise money for their risky ventures, and crazy prophets collect disciples, and quack healers obtain the confidence of patients. There is a glamour about these visionaries which infects those with whom they come in contact; and as the belief of those about us induces self-confidence as surely as their distrust chills us, a circuit of action and reaction is set up which, like what is popularly called a vicious circle, increases in strength as it proceeds. It is a true saying that nothing succeeds like success.

What modern psychology calls the language of unconscious gesture is an extraordinarily eloquent thing, and is interpreted by the subconsious minds of others and reacted to in a way that neither they nor we realize in the very least. When our subconscious gestures announce that we expect a welcome, that we expect unquestioning acquiescence, nine people out of ten will respond and give us what we subconsciously signal that we are expecting. If our self-doubtings cause us to signal our diffidence, we are simply "asking for trouble." If, on the other hand, our habitual day-dreams have been concerned with our triumphant successes, we hang out unconscious banners of triumph, and nine out of ten persons will line up and march behind them unless our lack of wisdom is such that we have chosen an impossible line of country. The mongrel that crawls up cringing is asking for the boot, but the boot is applied with discretion to the upstanding Alsatian.

CHAPTER IV

REMEMBERING PAST INCARNATIONS

NO sooner do people learn of the principles of reincarnation than they, not unnaturally, want to trace out their own karmic record in the past. We must not dismiss this desire as mere idle curiosity or foolish vanity, though it may contain elements of both these factors in varying proportions; it is a very useful thing to have some idea of one's past incarnations, but if this knowledge is to yield its full value, it is necessary that it should be first-hand, not second-hand; in other words, the actual recovery of past incarnations is an experience of altogether different calibre to having them read by a clairvoyant, however accurate. It is not without its value to have the record checked by a reliable clairvoyant, but the smallest fragment that we recover for ourselves is of infinitely greater value to us than the most accurate and complete record read off from the reflecting ether by another.

All the sting is gone from death the moment that we have glimpsed some authentic record of our personal past, for we know then, from personal experience, the immortality of the soul and its independence of bodily existence. It is well worth while to wait patiently till our own hands can draw back the curtain rather than have recourse to the clairvoyance of another, and so miss this great experience.

In order to unveil the past with accuracy, and with security from self-delusion, it is necessary to understand the basic principle of the doctrine of reincarnation. The esotericist recognizes two aspects of man, the Higher Self and the Lower Self. The Higher Self is a single, unified whole, which builds up around the Divine Spark, which is the nucleus of each human manifestation. The Lower Self is not a unified whole, but an ever-changing series of partial manifestations of the Higher Self, projected down into the planes of form and clothed upon with matter. The Higher Self is often spoken of as the Individuality, and each Lower Self as the Personality.

The word Individuality has for its root-meaning "that which cannot be divided," in other words, a unit. The word Personality is derived from the Latin *persona*, or mask. In ancient Greece the players in the sacred Mystery plays, which formed part of the Dionysiac Mysteries, always wore masks, which were conventional representations of the part they took. We can readily imagine the player, in the course of the play-cycle which formed part of the Mystery celebrations, assuming first one mask and then another as his parts changed with the play that was being performed. Thus do we conceive of the immortal soul in the Mysteries; we think of it as assuming first one personality, *persona*, or mask, after another as it plays its allotted part in the successive Mystery plays which form the changing cycle of spiritual experience.

At the end of each incarnation the form aspect of the *persona* disintegrates and returns as dust to dust according to its plane, for the ensouling life which built it up and which holds all together is withdrawn. First the body, then the etheric double, then the astral form, and finally the concrete mind, all go thus, dust to dust, back to the abyss of primordial matter whence they were wrought into living substance by the breath of life that ensouled them. Nothing remains of these, save the tracks in space which they wore by the habitual reactions of their nature. These are sometimes called the shadows on the Reflecting Ether.

It is not easy to understand an idea so foreign to our mundane experience, but if we think of the reflecting ether, or Akasha, which is the aura of the earth, as a sensitive plate upon which is photographed every reflection that has ever fallen upon it, and from which it is possible, by appropriate means, which will be considered later, to pick out and develop single impressions at will, we shall have a rough approximation to an understanding of the process. It is the reading of the Akashic Records that is done by clairvoyants when they look up the past for a client; but it is something quite different which we do for ourselves when we remember our own past incarnations, and it is this latter process which is of such value to us. It is much more likely to be these Akashic reflections which are dramatized by the subconscious mind of the medium than any actual return of the dead *in propria persona* when communication with the departed takes place. This is the weak spot in spiritualistic manifestations, and explains the trifling and fragmentary nature of so much that is communicated by the so-called spirits of the departed.

When we revive our own memories, however, a different process takes place, and this will best be understood if we carry our investigation of the processes of death a step farther.

As each of the four bodies of form disintegrates, its essential essence is absorbed by the immortal and eternal Higher Self or Individuality of the person. It is this absorption which, by withdrawing the higher principles, in fact causes the dissolution of the subtler form-bodies after the physical vehicle, their essential instrument of manifestation and means of experience, is rendered unfit for use, either by age, accident, or disease.

It will be seen from this that the actual form aspect of each incarnation is dissolved and done with after each incarnation, but that its essential essence, the ripe fruit of experience, is absorbed by the Higher Self. Thus does the Higher Self grow and evolve. It might aptly be said that the soul grazes in the fields of earth, and lies down to chew the cud beside the still waters of Heaven.

It follows, then, that the only thing that persists, incarnation after incarnation, is the spiritual principle, the ethical essence, extracted from the sum total of the experiences of each earth-life; the life itself and its memories going into the discard after it has, as it were, been sucked dry by the soul, which requires of it only this spiritual essence for its nutriment.

Let us now study the way in which memory is evoked. We can learn a great deal about this by observing what happens when we try to recite a poem of which we have not got too distinct a recollection. We know how hopeless it is to make a start unless someone can prompt us to the first line. Once we have that, off we go gaily, the poem unwinding itself spontaneously out of our subconscious memory until the thread of association breaks and we are once more in need of the indispensable help of the prompter if we are to start off afresh.

Stored in the Akasha, or Reflecting Ether, as previously described, are the memories of everything that has ever happened within the earth-sphere. If we can by any means secure the "prompt" to any particular set of memories, we can unwind them out of the aspect of sub-consciousness in ourselves which corresponds to the Akasha. We have, of course, a natural link in connection with anything that happened in one of our own previous incarnations. We cannot, however, pick this up on the planes of form, that is, of the concrete mind, by taking conscious thought, because there is no direct link between one incarnation and another on the planes of form; but we can pick it up via the Higher Self if we are able to think with the higher type of mentation, even if it be only for a brief flash.

In order to achieve this, we must consider our present

life as a whole, and see if we can discern any recurring problem in it; for such a problem will probably be due to karmic causes. Consequently it will have its root in past incarnations, and we can use it as a guide-rope to cross the gulf fixed in the continuity of consciousness by each experience of death that we have undergone. It will thus be seen that we have followed this guide-rope up onto the level of the Higher Self by meditating upon the abstract essence of the experiences we have recognized to be karmic, that is, to be the immediate outcome of past lives. Our next problem is to follow our guide-rope down again onto the planes of form at a diverging angle from normal consciousness.

CHAPTER V

REMEMBERING PAST INCARNATIONS
—continued

THE translation of consciousness from one plane to another is best achieved by availing ourselves of the resources placed at our disposal by the simple and universal experience of sleep, when the normal concrete consciousness is in abeyance, the five physical senses are closed down, and subconsciousness, with all it contains, is left unguarded and undisciplined for a space.

After the light is extinguished, let us sink deeply into meditation on the spiritual essence that we have divined as being at the root of the particular set of karmic experiences we have selected for examination, but let us carefully refrain from dwelling upon these experiences in any shape or form; and let us equally carefully refrain from passing any moral judgment on them, or formulating any good resolutions arising out of them. We must simply think of these experiences as the food of the soul, and as teaching it certain lessons.

Let us continue like this, between sleeping and waking, making no effort of the will to keep ourselves awake, until fragments and flashes of pictures begin to rise in the imagination. These the orthodox scientist calls hypnogogics, and has little realization of their significance, nor of the uses to which they can be put. We should never strain after these pictures, nor make any conscious effort to formulate them. They must arise spontaneously if they are to be of anv use to us. Let us remember that the skill in the use of this method lies in catching the impressions which are available to us as the mind crosses over from one state of consciousness to another and the two levels are momentarily blended. Then we are, in the words of astrology, on the cusp of consciousness and subconsciousness.

We must always bear in mind the fact that the impressions that have value are the spontaneous ones, because these alone well up from subconsciousness; the willed and directed ones are of the conscious mind, and these have no particular interest for us because we can command them at will. Consequently, let us have patience with ourselves, and remember that there is a knack to be acquired in the recovery of those impressions perceived when two opposite doors of the chambers of the mind happen to be open simultaneously. The trick lies in sliding easily and effortlessly from one state of consciousness to another with the mind's eyes open. It is a trick that has to be learnt, like the art of balancing on a bicycle, and we must be content to try many times, with the most fragmentary results before we can count upon getting anything worth having, though in some cases it may occasionally be that immediate results are obtained because the memories happen to be lying near the surface; but these are rare. When a definite reincarnation memory is obtained it is usually recognized by the emotion that surrounds it. We may see a perfect phantasmagoria of the past floating before the mind's eye as we lie between sleeping and waking in the darkness and silence, but it will have no special significance for us beyond that of a generalised beauty and interest. But when a fragment of one of our own authentic memories crops up, it will bring with it all its attendant emotional association, even if it be no more than a glimpse of the wall of a house where our physical tenement once dwelt. It is this uprush of emotion that tells us that we are on the right track.

The moment this occurs, we ought to rouse ourselves and concentrate on this fragment, so that we shall ensure that it shall not sink back again into subconsciousness and be lost to us. It is a good plan to have paper and pencil beside the bed, and to turn on the light and make notes or a rough sketch. In so doing we shall probably sacrifice a night's sleep, for these memories of the past are upheaving things when they reappear; but they need not necessarily be painful things: it may, in fact, be the fascination of them that drives sleep away for some hours.

Therefore, together with the writing materials to record the experience, we should also have the means of a light meal, such as biscuits and milk, in order that the gates may be closed again when the opening has been explored, for there is no formula so effective for closing the gates of consciousness as a little food in the stomach, especially hot food.

Next day we ought to try and ascertain to what period of history and to what country the fragment we have recaptured belongs, and then soak ourselves in the literature of that period and country. To this end historical novels are very useful, for they help us most effectually to see the past as a living human experience, and not as a dry-as-dust record in a museum. To this end we should also try to obtain illustrations of this epoch and place; and especially to see, and if possible handle, the actual relics of it such as may be found in museums. If we can by any fortunate chance possess ourselves of some authentic relic of this past, which shall act as a magnetic link, our experiment is greatly simplified, and whatever we obtain will come with much greater vividness.

The imagination will gradually build up a picture of this time and place, and if we are wise we shall limit ourselves strictly to one incarnation at a time; for we shall not only become confused, but form a very bad psychic habit, if we let the pictures of two or more incarnations run together and superimpose themselves one on another, like two exposures on one plate of a camera.

When the conscious mind has supplied itself with the necessary furniture and properties, we shall find that the fragments of memory are beginning to use these symbols and pictures in order to clothe themselves with flesh and dwell among us, as it were. In other words, the conscious mind is using these symbols and pictures to give form to the intangible impressions that are rising to the surface of the subconscious mind under the invocation of our interest and desire. We shall always know any genuine memory by the emotion it evokes.

Once a definite set of memories has begun to formulate itself into something coherent, we shall find comparatively little difficulty in applying the method to incarnation after incarnation; though we shall always find it easier to get the memories of incarnations when the body was of the same sex as the present one than to recall memories of incarnations when it was of the opposite sex. When we have gained proficiency in the method, however, it is a valuable experience to force the mind to recall memories of incarnations in a body of the opposite sex to that which we now occupy, for it gives a great expansion of consciousness and understanding, and is an experience never to be forgotten.

CHAPTER VI

WORKING OUT KARMA

THE word Karma is borrowed from the Eastern Tradition, but it is so widely used that it has become incorporated in the English language. The term used in the Western Tradition to describe the same influence is Destiny; but the Eastern word being more familiar, we will adhere to it in these pages.

Karma, or Destiny, is the influence of past lives as it affects our present life. It shows itself in two ways: in environment and in character. Our environmental karma determines the circumstances into which we shall be born and the congenital dispositions of the body with which we are born; for the body is just as much the environment of the soul as the home is the environment of the body. Temperament is not the same thing as character, for temperament is determined by the Ray-influence prevailing in the cosmic atmosphere at the time when the Divine Spark, which is the nucleus of the soul, began to be separated out from the formless mass of the Life-wave. Fundamental temperament is constant throughout the whole evolution of the Divine Spark, but character changes with every incarnation, and even in the course of an incarnation as experience works upon the personality. Character, in fact, may be defined as temperament modified by experience.

We come into incarnation, then, with a particular type of basic temperament which cannot be altered, but only developed and harmonized. In other words, we can be a good specimen or a poor specimen of our type, but one cannot make fish of flesh. The fundamental character of the personality in each incarnation is the result of the bias that the basic temperament has acquired in the course of its experiences in previous lives.

The greater part of karma works out by means of

character, not by means of drastic happenings which are specially dealt to us out of the blue, as it were. If we observe the lives of others closely, we shall be able to trace this, though we may not see it so clearly in our own lives, which come too near our hearts for us to be able to see them in impartial perspective.

Allowing for the influence of the environment into which we are born and our congenital health, character exercises the predominant selective influence in determining the course of our lives. According to our character do we react to conditions; we choose when the choice is offered us; we dominate or submit; direct or are driven. To either alternative of a pair of alternatives there hangs a long train of consequences. It will be seen, therefore, that the course of our lives is continually being biased in the same direction by our temperament and character.

Let me illustrate this by an example. A person may be of the dynamic, power-loving, ruling type; this is his basic temperament, determined by the Ray-influence that prevailed when his soul started off on its evolutionary journey. In this incarnation, however, there is a streak of laziness in him. In consequence of this he will be continually failing to grasp opportunity, either because he is disinclined to exert himself when opportunity comes along, or because he has failed to prepare himself to take advantage of it.

Such a man's life will be a tragic record of disappointments, capacities that never had their opportunity to display themselves, lack of recognition and appreciation.

His misfortunes may truly be said to be due to karmic causes, and these will undoubtedly show in the horoscope; but shall we say that it is circumstances which have dealt his karma to that man, or shall we say that it is his character that has dealt it to him?

The following test will show which it is. If he changes his character, a change in his karma will follow. If he becomes diligent instead of slothful, the next opportunity that comes along will not be missed, and so his luck will turn.

We do not appreciate the extent to which character deals out karma because it does it so subtly. It is the little foxes that get the opportunity to spoil the vines. Faults of character are not the only little foxes we have to reckon with; judgment plays an even more important part in determining the course of our fate; for it is possible to find a man with a very faulty character who has excellent judgment, and he will flourish like a green bay-tree.

Faulty judgment, however, rests at bottom on faults of character. There are errors of judgment which are due to impulsiveness, for we do not take sufficient trouble to ascertain the facts and think things out; other errors are due to our dislike of facing unpleasant facts, and so leaving them out of our calculations; vanity may lead us to over-estimate our own capacities and under-estimate the forces arrayed against us; lack of sympathy and imagination may cause us to fail to realize the kind of reaction we shall stir up in others by the things we do and the way we do them; laziness may lead to shirking, and get caught out; carelessness to lack of attention to detail; cruelty and unscrupulousness may array all sorts of resentments against us so that folk go out of their way to do us an ill turn; all these things are causes which we have set going with our own hands, but the results appear to come to us out of our environment; and yet they are simply due to the way in which our environment is reacting to us, which is a thing we generally leave out of our calculations when distributing the blame for the untoward occurrences that beset us.

A woman, for instance, complains, and not without reason, of her bad husband. But there must have been something unworthy in her to have been attracted by an unworthy mate. If people prefer pinchbeck gold to honest copper, they must not be surprised if the world breaks their false coin in half and throws the pieces back at them.

Let us accept as our basic fact that 90 per cent. of karma comes to us by means of the reactions our environment makes to our way of dealing with it. When we set out to work off our karma, it is character wholly and solely that we work upon. If we can change our character, we can change our karma; for the selective bias will then alter its direction and environment will react to us differently.

The bias of a character is due to what is left over after the different influences in the last life have cancelled each other out in purgatory. Our good intention will weigh in the balance against our broken resolutions; our self-indulgences will detract from our capacities. Our struggles with our weaknesses will tell in the scales against the influence of those weaknesses, and these will have less power over us when we come into incarnation again. What is left over after this purgatorial process is completed gives us our bias in our next incarnation.

The aim of evolution is to develop perfect specimens of each type. We are not expected to change our type, but to harmonize it. One man may be the perfected administrator; another the perfected artist; another the perfected priest; but it is unwise to ask your artist to be an administrator: or your administrator to be a priest, for then we get princes of the Church who serve the Prince of this world.

Whatever is good in us is due to the basic temperament expressing itself in harmonized balance; whatever is bad is due to a bias of character. Our good karma is given us through our temperament, which is aligned to its own type of cosmic force; our evil karma comes to us through a tangle of forces setting up conflict when we are out of alignment with cosmic force. Therefore it is always unsatisfactory to allow any one else to determine our ideals for us, for they are liable to drive square pegs into round holes. We have got to feel our way towards righteousness by means of wisdom. There is no quality which is a virtue in itself. We might as well say that because a teaspoonful of a certain medicine did us good, a teacupful will do us more good. This does not necessarily follow, as we can easily prove for ourselves.

Patience and meekness enhance the vices of the coward; courage and energy render more dangerous the vices of the bully. Even love can be misplaced and overdone, and degenerate into emotional self-indulgence and silliness.

In view of all this, what can we do to work out our karma from the practical and immediate standpoint?

If our evil karma is due to a bias of character towards one side, it follows that if we can correct that bias, we shall correct that karma. A bias can be corrected, firstly, by steadily neutralizing it and building up the opposite qualities by means of meditation; and secondly, by altering our attitude towards life by the same means, and bringing ourselves into line with the cosmic forces of our Ray instead of getting athwart them and being swirled into eddy and backwash by contending forces.

CHAPTER VII

WORKING OUT KARMA—*continued*

WE have seen the way in which karma determines character; and character, by determining the way in which we treat our environment, influences profoundly the way in which our environment treats us. In other words, our good and evil fortune depend to a very much greater extent than we realize upon the reactions our environment makes to our behaviour.

There is, however, another factor in karma to be reckoned with; the factor which most people think to be the whole of karma, though we have tried to show that this is not the case; this factor might very well be termed predestination in the good old-fashioned sense. Our way in life lies by a certain path leading through desert, mountain, or meadow as the case may be; and though our feeling towards that path are the predominating factor in determining our happiness or unhappiness thereon, and even our health—for we may approach the mountain road in the spirit of the mountaineer or the laden mule—nevertheless, we have no choice in the path by which we must go, and must take it as we find it and make either the best or worst of it according to our nature.

We have seen that it is possible to change our attitude towards life to a profound degree, and thereby to modify our karma; but we may well ask how a hard karma can be made endurable when, being predestined, it permits of no modification? We come now to the root of the whole problem: the only approach to the working out of our karma. It may seem a hard saying to many, but the fact must be faced that karma is a thing to be accepted, not eluded.

This is the key to the whole problem. Karma must not only be accepted as inevitable, it must actually be welcomed as a scholarship in the school of life. When we have arrived at this attitude towards our karma its working out has begun. This does not mean, however, that it will set us no more problems, submit us to no more tests; we do not avoid karma by working it out; we come to the end of it by getting through it. We might just as well expect to be spared further lessons in arithmetic because we have got a sum right.

When an initiate sets out to work out his karma, he deliberately invokes it and speeds it up. The immediate result of this is twofold. Firstly, a crisis in his affairs; and secondly, a sudden access of power to deal with that crisis. After this critical period has been passed through, no more karma is left for him to work out, and he can truly say that all things work together for good for them that love God, for his good karma is now working unchecked; for the powers gained by him in the working-out remain, whereas the resistances have been overcome. He then experiences the curious opening-up of the way which is so often met with by those who make the unreserved dedication.

In dealing with our predestined karma, therefore, we should make a virtue of necessity and accept it cheerfully, trying to see what lessons it has to teach us, what characteristics it is designed to develop in us, and actively and intelligently co-operate with the discipline of life in learning those lessons and developing those characteristics.

We should lift our eyes above the sea of troubles and gaze upon the ideal of perfected character. Let us imagine ourselves as we shall be when perfected by life after life of steadfast dedication—strong, wise, harmonized, perfectly poised amid the ups and downs of life as a skilful rider controls a spirited horse, giving easily to its curvetings, yet directing and controlling it. With this ideal in mind, let us consider impersonally the difficulties that surround us and see how perfected wisdom, strength, and love would enable us to rise above them and work them out; then let us see how these very difficulties are developing in us the characteristics we need for our perfecting.

If we would look upon life as a school and try to understand its lessons, how differently it would appear to us to what it does when we look upon it as an affliction—and how differently we should be able to deal with it!

It is open to anyone who can rise above a self-centred attitude to do what the initiate does, and invoke the Lords of Karma. Before he ventures upon this, however, he must have reached the point in spiritual development where he desires the good rather than the pleasant—the ideal of perfected character in preference to the pleasure-pain principle. When his heart is really turned towards the ideal, the Dark Angel which according to Cabalistic tradition stands behind his left shoulder, becomes an initiator and shows him the Path.

In the language of the Mysteries, initiation by the Dark Angel follows upon the invocation of the Lords of Karma, and is the quickest and surest way to find the Path. Those who have taken this initiation come onto the Path karma-free. According to Mystery tradition, the initiator always comes when called and asks us for the pass-word, and if we can give that pass-word we are admitted to the Temple of the Mysteries. We do not realize, however, that it is life itself which is the Great Initiator, and that the physical ceremony only ratifies the spiritual experience.

When we experience a whole-souled desire for the Way of Perfection, life always comes and asks us a test question. All those who have come by the Path tell us that immediately upon the formulation of this desire came a testing experience in the ordinary way of life. If they were able to apply spiritual principles to the working out of this experience, they had answered the test question correctly, and passed within the Veil; thenceforward they see all life in terms of spiritual principle instead of physical sensation.

There is no mystery about the pass-word with which we must answer the Dark Angel of affliction, who comes to us in the name of the Lord—every great spiritual teacher who has come to mankind has told us what this pass-word is. It was uttered by Our Lord at the supreme testing in the Garden of Gethsemane—"Not my will, but Thine be done." When we come to the point when we can say this in answer to the dark messenger of affliction that the Lords of Karma will send to question us when we invoke them, we shall hear the answering Word—"Well done, good and faithful servant, enter ye into the joy of your Lord."

It is the unreserved acceptance of our fate as the particular lesson we need for our spiritual development that is the key which unlocks the gate of our karmic bondage. When karma is accepted it is more than half overcome. We should make it our immediate aim to achieve serenity, and even happiness, under whatever circumstances the Lords of Karma may elect to send us. When they see that we have achieved serenity they will say, "This lesson is learnt; it need not be repeated." As long as any experience has power to disturb us, we have not mastered it, and it will be repeated life after life until the lesson it has to teach is mastered.

The aim of karma is not to break us, but to make us. We need never fear that karma will be piled on karma until we are broken. It is never karma that breaks us; if we are broken it is because we have broken ourselves against it. Those who have seen wild ponies off the moors being broken to harness know something of the viewpoint of the Lords of Karma. As the fighting, stupid, vicious pony appears to the onlooking humans, so do we appear to the Lords of Karma.

The great majority of human beings are well-intentioned. The problem of the Lords of Karma is not so much to eradicate active evil as to get their pupils to understand what is required of them, for we are just as much a lower order of creation to them as the animals are to us. Let us look upon the buffetings of fate as the barkings, and if need be the shrewd nippings of the sheepdog, and the stick-wavings and shouts of the shepherd trying to induce us to enter the green pastures awaiting us, and cease to consider them as the blind thwartings of our legitimate desires by an unkind Fate.

When we utter those mightiest of all the Words of Power, "Not my will, but Thine be done," we come automatically into line with cosmic force, and this new will in us is no longer thwarted, but carried swiftly to its goal by the tides of the spiritual universe. This will, however, is the will to spiritual perfection; it does not gratify either our vanity or our greed; nor will it shelter our cowardice or sloth. The path by which it leads us will wind uphill all the way, but it will be sunlit and serene, and we shall never lack shelter for the night.

CHAPTER VIII

DIVINATION : ITS USES AND LIMITS

DIVINATION is really a spiritual diagnosis whereby we try to discover what subtle influences are at work in our affairs. It can be exceedingly helpful if rightly done; but it can be exceedingly harmful if improperly done because of the depressing suggestion and sowing of unwarranted suspicion to which it can give rise.

A divination should be regarded as a weather-vane which shows which way the winds of the invisible forces are blowing; but it should always be remembered that a weather-vane is not meant to determine the course that a ship is to take; it merely indicates how best to trim the sails.

There are two types of divination, one of which is purely psychic, relying upon vision or communication from spirits, and employing at most a crystal or a pool of ink to aid vision. The other type makes use of a set of arbitrary symbols, such as playing cards, or the prick-figures of geomancy, and reads the significance of the chance dealing of these according to a definite code, thus considerably reducing, but by no means eliminating, the personal factor.

Anyone with practical experience of seership knows that to try to obtain enlightenment by psychic means concerning any matter in which one has a strong emotional bias is seldom satisfactory, for the bias vitiates the results to such a degree that they may prove most misleading. It is well known that no seer can skry for himself in any matter in which he himself is intimately concerned. This is even true when resort is had to another psychic; for the strong emotion in the mind of the querent is very apt to influence the psychic unconsciously, so that the results obtained may either be coloured by desire, or, if the influence is unconsciously resisted, may lean to the other extreme.

The best thing to do under such circumstances is to employ one of the methods of divination in which the symbols employed are shaken together and dealt out by chance. Of these the Tarot is far and away the best, because much the most subtle and comprehensive, and those who possess the higher understanding can obtain an insight into the spiritual factors in the case under investigation.

To use the Tarot properly, however, requires a very great deal of preparation, and the preparation does not consist merely in a knowledge of the significance of the cards, but in getting in touch with the forces behind the cards. An adequate rule-of-thumb use of it, however, can be made by any sincere person for himself, though it is doubtful if he could use it satisfactorily for anyone else.

Obtain a *new* pack of Tarot cards, for a used one will be too full of other people's magnetism to be reliable, and carry them on the person, and sleep with them under the pillow, and handle them and ponder upon the meaning of the pictures in the light of what the book of instructions has to say about them until the significance of each picture is realized. It does not matter greatly which pack is used, whether the quaint, hideous, archaic ones, or the very beautiful ones redrawn in recent times for Mr. A. E. Waite; it is not the details of the cards that matter, but that they should serve as reminders, as it were, of the ideas underlying them. As soon as one perceives some sort of significance in the picture on a card, one has made a link with that card, and its appearance in the divination will mean something.

Having got in touch with one's chosen pack, the next thing is to lay out a divination according to whatever system is chosen, work it out according to the book, and note down the results obtained and the position in which the cards fell. Repeat the process a second time, and a third time, upon each occasion keeping accurate notes of the fall of the cards, and, of course, thoroughly shuffling the cards between each lay-out. If certain cards keep on coming up, and especially if they come up in approximately the same positions, or even if cards of the same type predominate through the three divinations, it may safely be concluded that the system is working satisfactorily, and a divination may be made on the basis of the recurring cards. But if the three divinations bear no resemblance to each other; if even the balance of the four suits does not remain constant for at least two out of the three, and if none of the Greater Trumps turn up more than once, then it must be concluded that the Tarot is not working for the diviner, and the divination should be abandoned. The same principles apply if divinations are done with ordinary playing-cards, though this method is not nearly so sensitive and comprehensive as Tarot divinations.

Divination is a thing that cannot be learnt out of books, but builds up gradually as a system of associated ideas in the mind of the operator. Moreover, one varies very much in one's capacity for divination; upon one occasion one may be absolutely inspired, the cards recur and recur, and one reads with the most extraordinary insight, one thing leading to another in an endless train; at another time, one may have to spell out the meaning of the lay-out with reference to the book for almost every card. It will always be found that it is useless to force a divination; if the interpretation does not leap spontaneously to the mind it is unlikely to contain much insight.

Far better results can be obtained in this way than by going to dubious professionals. The only person who can do better for one than one can do for oneself is an initiate who has specialized in the Tarot; these, however, will never do the work for a fee, and therefore it is only under special circumstances that one can obtain such a reading.

All visions and voices that are heard when one is under strain should be highly suspect, for even if they spoke the truth they would be unwholesome symptoms, indicating that the mind is tending to come apart, to dissociate, under the strain. Every experienced occultist always closes down all supernormal faculties when conditions are adverse, because he knows that the still small voice is never heard in the thunder or the whirlwind, but only in the silence. The higher contacts give a sense of power, of protection, of peace; they do not speak with voices. It can never be said too often that whenever the Unseen becomes visible to the physical eye, or audible to the physical ear, something is going wrong with the works, for the planes are leaking the one into the other and unless the leakage can be stopped, mental unbalance will result.

Even to see with the inner eye, and hear with the inner ear, realizing all the time that the impressions are subjective, needs caution; the greatest safeguard we can have in the use of any psychic powers we may possess is to understand the psychology of them, and keep constantly in mind the fact that what we are perceiving is not the thing itself, but a dream-like cartoon of it that is being dramatized by our subconscious minds.

The further we advance in our spiritual development, the less difference will there be between the operation of our higher consciousness and our normal mentality. Seership is an illuminated state of the normal mind in which discernment is raised to a very high degree. The more primitive and unevolved the nature, the more startling and abnormal the phenomena.

The problem of the horoscope is a very perplexing one. A horoscope can be a very great help; it can also be a most pernicious influence, full of poisonous suggestions. Everything depends upon the wisdom and spiritual quality of the astrologer. The right kind of astrologer can be as helpful as the right kind of priest. Let it be remembered, however, that the professional, advertising astrologer is obliged to do an enormous amount of hack-work and it is almost impossible for him to keep his spiritual virginity. Moreover, no well-known astrologer, with a large practice, can do personally all the horoscopes he receives; the work is farmed out. You are more likely to receive good value from a friend who is studying astrology for its own sake than from the professional who is grinding out horoscopes all day long for a living, and who may be at the third or fourth remove from the celebrity to whom you sent your guinea.

Professional occultism, which is a breach of the very basis of the spiritual sciences, is a sordid and unsatisfactory business, which blesses neither those who do it nor those who have it done. I have never seen anything but harm come from running round from one soothsayer to another; nor anyone who made a living out of it and kept their spiritual powers unimpaired.

CHAPTER IX

THE USE AND ABUSE OF MIND POWER

IT is by no means simple to find a standard by which to judge the limits of the justifiable use of occult knowledge. There is a borderline of use and abuse of which common sense and common honesty must form the touchstone, but it may be possible to lay down certain rules to help in arriving at a judgment in individual cases. We can at least hope to find a middle way between the extremes indicated by the advertisements of certain transatlantic organizations upon the one hand, and the doctrine that an initiate may never make use of occult power for his own personal ends upon the other.

The more blatant of the get-what-you-want courses in spiritual development are of such a nature that even the advertisements find it difficult to justify them, and one marvels that a sufficient number of sufficiently silly persons can be found to make them pay.

One also marvels that the *ipse dixit* adepts can get people to believe them when they say that their omission to make use of their powers on their own behalf is due to the strictness of their principles. "Physician, heal thyself," is a not unreasonable test to impose on our spiritual pastors and masters.

The notion that the more spiritual one is, the more poverty-stricken one should be is derived from the East, as is much of our religious ethics ; and because the temperament, physical conditions, and climate of India and Palestine, the chief sources of our spiritual inspiration, are entirely different from our own, some of the accepted precepts are by common consent given no more than lip-service because they prove impractical for men and women of Nordic race in a cold climate.

This is not a good thing for the spiritual morale of a race. If it is so generally agreed that certain commandments are so impractical that they can be ignored without incurring social odium, the whole basis of dogmatic morality becomes suspect, and its writ ceases to run outside the inner circle of ascetics. What we need is an ethical standard that shall do justice between man and man and spur the soul forward on its evolutionary path.

Let us realize first of all that there are two ways in which esoteric knowledge can be used in order to "better ourselves" materially. It is possible to influence the minds and wills of our fellow-men so that they shall give us what we want ; it is also possible to draw directly from the great cosmic reservoirs of undifferentiated force. The former way is the way of Black Magic; the latter is the way of White Magic. An operation, then, passes the first test when it does no harm to any creature; for if it is axiomatic that we have no right to interfere with the free-will and responsibility of any soul, even for his own good, save in an emergency, how much less have we the right to try to influence any one for our own good?

Jesus said, "I am come that they might have life, and that they might have it more abundantly." This should be the keynote of our operations to secure better material conditions by mental and spiritual means. We should seek the spiritual sources of life and drink therefrom. This we do by means of meditation performed upon the Great Unmanifest, the Source of all Being; realizing its infinity, omnipotence, and eternal duration. The source of our being is in this ever-outpouring, infinite energy; the amount of this energy we receive is limited solely by our capacity for realization; if we can increase our realization and get rid of our inhibitions, we correspondingly increase our intake of cosmic energy, and this energy is transmuted within our being into all the different forms of activity that go to make up human life.

If our vital energy goes up, every factor in our nature is quickened and intensified; the artist paints with new power and inspiration; the insight of the scientist is redoubled; the skill and strength of the manual worker are increased; the intelligence and happiness of a child—the beauty and charm of a woman—whatever we are becomes intensified. This, in fact, is the real basis of spiritual healing—the true spiritual healing as distinguished from healing by suggestion; the *vis medicatrix naturae*, which is the only real curative agent, becomes greatly increased, and, thus increased, can often ameliorate, and sometimes completely cure conditions that previously resisted it.

We must realize, however, that the action of the inpouring cosmic force is not selective; every aspect of our nature is intensified by its influence; consequently, whatever is unregenerate comes up immediately in an acute form, and unless we can pass safely through the spiritual crisis that always ensues in some form or another when spiritual power is called down, our last state will be considerably worse than our first. The Christian Scientists, who have a wider experience than anyone else of mind-healing, call this crisis "Chemicalization," and always watch out for it in treating their patients and regard it as a sign that the treatment is proving effectual.

If we are working upon right lines, however, the crisis is minimised, for the true line of approach to the source of spiritual power is in the spirit of the words, " Not my will, but Thine be done." There are two methods of drawing down this power—the ceremonial one and the meditative one. The ceremonial one should only be used for concentrating the power that has already been contacted by meditative means; it is a method only suited to the advanced worker, who has been disciplined and purified; we need not therefore consider it in these pages, save to warn against its use, as in inexpert hands it can produce disastrous results. The meditative method consists in increasing awareness by means of contemplation of symbols of infinity, eternity, and omnipotence, affirming and reaffirming the perfect harmony of cosmic law, and picturing our own relationship to that which we are contemplating. With increasing realization there comes increasing vitality, mental capacity, and poise. Upon this basis of increased capacity and poise all else is built up. If what we need is more money, we will soon find we can earn more because our market value as human beings has gone up. If what we want is work, we shall find little difficulty in obtaining an engagement because everyone we come in contact with will sense unconsciously the vitality and serenity that animates us. If we have life-problems to work out, we shall find that increased serenity lessens our reactions to them, and when we cease to react, we cease to stir them up; our increasing vitality gives us more energy and courage with which to deal with them; our increased mental capacity gives us increased insight with which to solve them; and one thing leading to another, "all things work together for good to them that love God."

This is the only right and proper method of using occult power for our own purposes; and it would be difficult to see what ethical objection could be advanced against such use for legitimate ends; for not only does it defraud no man, but increases our spiritual stature and advances us upon the evolutionary path.

Our next problem is to consider what are legitimate ends. We may safely say that whatever brings harmony where there was disharmony leads to a legitimate end. This may sound a very simple and satisfactory solution of all our problems. We have merely to make up our minds what we want and go ahead and get it.

But it is not quite as simple as all that. What we may need to make us happy is not more money, or the love of some particular person, but an entire change of attitude towards life; for if our attitude to life is basically wrong we shall reverse the process of the Midas touch and turn everything we handle to dross.

The only safe thing to do when we want our problems straightened out is to surrender ourselves unreservedly to cosmic law and determine to do the right thing, whatever it costs. When we do this we come down to bedrock, and whatever is built then stands on a firm foundation; but however much cosmic power we call down, we cannot build an enduring dwelling on foundations of sand.

We must never consider expediency when we are working by means of cosmic force; let us learn to trust in its infinity and omnipotence, and rely upon being able to call down sufficient force to do whatever is needful to bring all things to a just and harmonious conclusion.

There is one point that recurs so often in the questions asked by students that it is well to deal with it specifically. How far is it justifiable to use this method for obtaining money? Here again a great deal must be left to a conscience enlightened by common sense. We may safely say, however, that it is never wise to work for a specific sum of money. By so doing we limit the whole range and scope of opportunities that might otherwise have been available for us. Supposing, for instance, we worked for a hundred pounds, which we conceived to be the sum necessary to solve our immediate problems, and having obtained the cosmic contacts, a hundred pounds came our way (and it is surprising the exactness with which sums of money can be obtained in this manner, neither more nor less), it might quite well have been that our realization and invocation would have sufficed not merely to get us out of our immediate difficulty, but to change the whole course of our lives; we have got our hundred pounds, it is true, but what of the opportunities that were inhibited by the limits we imposed on the operations of infinity? If we have been able to set in motion cosmic power sufficient to produce a hundred pounds, we have started off a chain of causes that might have led anywhere if we had not checked them at the hundred pound limit.

We are very unwise to outline our askings when we approach the Source of All Life. Rather should we ask for harmony and increasing fullness of life, and leave it to Infinite Wisdom to discern our real needs; for needs and wants are not always the same thing. In nine cases out of ten a change of heart is needed as well as change of circumstances before harmony can come in; and in a goodly proportion of those cases a change of heart is all that is needed, and the circumstances will do well enough when we approach them properly.

We make a fundamental error when we try to obtain happiness by the possession of things. Seek first the Kingdom of Heaven which is within us, and all these things that make for happiness shall be added unto us through a thousand unexpected channels till they are more than we can ask or think.

But as it is obvious that money is the key to so much in this world, and that although the possession of it cannot give us happiness, the lack of it can make it exceedingly difficult for us to be happy, we must squarely face the problem as to how far we may expect fullness of life to express itself in the form of more abundant money. We know well what all the great religious teachers have had to say about money, and how scantily equipped they were with this world's goods; we also know that our Lord said that it was easier for a camel to pass through the eye of a needle than for a rich man to enter the Kingdom of Heaven. In the face of all this, are we right in regarding money as a legitimate need for which we may use spiritual forces without injuring ourselves spiritually?

The key to this problem lies, I think, in the realization that it is the simplicity of life which comes through a realization of what are the essentials and what are the inessentials that is the one thing needful; for the needs of this essential simplicity I believe we may justifiably invoke spiritual aid. This simplicity should include orderliness, seemliness and beauty, and the recreation that keeps the balance of our natures intact. It should also include scope for the development of our capacities. I cannot conceive, however, that it should include luxury or display, or enable us to put our neighbours in the shade.

If we value spiritual things, this will be our natural mode of living, for we shall not want to be distracted by the much care that goes with much cattle. If we have not got the roots of spiritual realization in us, we had better leave spiritual power alone, for the first thing it does when it visits us is to burn up the dross in our natures, and if the proportion of dross to pure gold is too high, the consequences may not be all we had hoped for. One must have the right kind of desires before one can safely trust spiritual forces for their fulfilment. In any case, we must always be prepared to offer a greater or lesser change of heart as our contribution to the task.

CHAPTER X

ETHERIC MAGNETISM

OUR knowledge of electricity is of comparatively recent development; and although extensive practical applications have been made of this elusive energy, we are still ignorant concerning its real nature. Recent advances in knowledge, however, have shown us that its distribution is much wider-spread than had previously been recognized; in fact, we might safely say that electricity is all-pervasive, and it only requires the development of instruments of sufficient sensitiveness to demonstrate the fact.

It had long been known that the human body was of the nature of an electric battery; that nervous impulses were transmitted by means of weak electric currents running along the nerve fibres, and that the electrical conductivity of the body changed with the change of emotional states. Recent discovery has produced an instrument of such sensitiveness that not only can it demonstrate that the human body gives off electrical energy, but can actually measure the amount—greater and less in different individuals—finding it to be the greatest in young, virile males, and least in the elderly and those in weak health.

A wide range of experimental work opens up along these lines, and it will be interesting to see how closely it agrees with the traditions of esoteric science. For this electrical energy of the human body has long been known to initiates, although other names have been given to it than those that modern science is coining to fit the facts that are coming to light, and it is well known to be the basis of much occult phenomena.

Its practical applications in our daily lives are fairly widely realized; but unfortunately the value of this knowledge has been vitiated by the amount of superstition and auto-suggestion that have grown up around it. We need to find the middle way between a stubborn disregard of all subtle influences that exposes us to much needless discomfort, or even more serious harm, and a hyper-suggestible faddiness that ends in hypochondriasis.

Because we recognize the actuality of an influence, it does not follow that we must forthwith surrender to it. There are two ways in which we should react to it; firstly, by learning all we can about it and making use of it medicinally, as it were; learning its indications and dosage, and how to direct and control its activities. And secondly, by learning how to neutralise or deflect it if its influences under certain conditions should be found deleterious.

Experimental science has now caught up with esoteric tradition in asserting that every living creature is an electric battery, and has learnt to measure the electrical energy quantitatively; the next step will be the demonstration of the varying qualitative nature of the electrical energy generating by that living battery. This diversity of quality esoteric science clearly recognizes, and classifies under the seven planetary influences, using various divinatory methods as tests and indicators. By these means a rough approximation can be arrived at, though we shall have to wait for experimental science to give us precise methods of testing and measuring.

Meanwhile, however, we can take the esoteric doctrines as working hypotheses and show their practical application to our lives; a very small amount of experimenting along these lines will soon convince us of the actuality of the influences we are dealing with.

First and foremost, let us conceive of every form, whether animate or inanimate, as emanating a magnetic field of electrical energy. Then let us conceive of the exchange of magnetism between any objects that come within range of each others' electrical fields. Let us also remember that this magnetism varies in quality as well as in quantity, and that the variation depends upon the nature of the rhythm of its pulsating energies. It will follow then, that we are all the time receiving electro-magnetic influences of a very subtle nature from everything with which we come in contact, and from every person with whom we are in any sort of relationship. Equally it follows that all and each of these will be taking electrical energy from us according to their individual nature.

We must not, however, run away with the idea that all interchange of magnetic energies is of the nature of vampirism. This is far from being the case. To give and receive magnetism is normal to us, and the lack of such an interchange affects us as harmfully as the lack of the necessary vitamins—equally subtle and little-understood factors in the economy of living creatures.

There is a normal exchange of magnetism which is intensely stimulating, both to those who give and to those who receive; the breaking of this circuit produces distinct nervous pathologies which can only be cured by its restoration. This interchange can, however, be subject to certain pathologies, and these also we must consider in their place.

We can see both these aspects of magnetic influence clearly illustrated in the relationship between mother and child. A young child will not thrive without intimate personal love and contact with someone who cares for it as an individual. This is so well known that nowadays young children are never herded together in large orphanages, but farmed out in individual cottage homes in small groups; for it was found that the infant mortality in the mass rearing of babies was abnormally high, and the intelligence developing among them abnormally low.

So tangible is the influence of the magnetism of the mother that a well-known doctor recommends that a nervous, highly-strung mother should not hold her child in her arms, but support it on a cushion so as to insulate it from her disturbed magnetic influence.

The influence of the father is just as important as that

of the mother, but it does not reach the child directly during its earliest years, but comes to it through the mother. This has only to be pointed out to be recognized, for how different is the influence transmitted to her child by a woman happy and secure in her marriage from that transmitted by one who is uneasy and unhappy.

As the child grows older, however, it should normally outgrow the influence of the mother-magnetism and become receptive to the influence of the father-magnetism, which ushers it into the group mind of the race and makes it a regular member thereof. For just as the mother gives birth to a child as a separate physical individual, so the father gives birth to it as a social individual. We do not give sufficient importance to the part played by the race-life in our individual lives, nor recognize that man is a social animal, and that his group relationships are as much a part of his mental being as his other instincts.

In this social relationship, both mundane and psychological, the father is all-important. It is a great mistake to leave the children to the management of the mother after the nursery days are over. They are far better off under the discipline of the more rough-and-ready male, who does not fuss and fidget over trifles and gives a sound thrashing for serious offences, than in the over-sensitive and over-sensitizing hands of the female parent. More freedom and less tenderness are a better preparation for a life than the " mother-love " so often and so unwisely given. Mental specialists know well the results brought about by the over-prolonging of the sensitizing feminine magnetism and the consequent starvation of the invigorating male magnetism.

It is for this reason that the family and not the individual must always remain the prime social unit, and that the experiments in child-culture undertaken by the Soviet have had to be modified: it is for this reason also that free love is an impractical proposition because it produces homeless children, and a child never thrives outside a home. A home is as essential to a child as a nest to a bird. For in the home, and in the home alone, can he enjoy the right magnetic conditions for his development.

In the immediate magnetism of his mother's arms he receives essential spiritual vitamins during his earliest years. Later, in the atmosphere of his father's pride and protectiveness, he receives the influences essential for his development as a social being. Adequate substitutes are hard to find for these two personal relationships. The mother's is, perhaps, the easiest to replace, because most women get fond of any small child that is in their care. But the average man can seldom be got to feel any pride in someone else's offspring, and it is this family pride behind him which is such an invaluable support to an adolescent finding his place in the great world opening before him.

There is no substitute for the magnetism given off by happiness and affection, and pride and protection within a secure home circle, and children who have this start in life have an incalculable advantage over those who are born of contention. Moreover, they will tend to reproduce their own home conditions when they come to have a home and children of their own.

CHAPTER XI

ETHERIC MAGNETISM—*continued*

ETHERIC magnetism plays a very important part in the relationship between the sexes. We usually think of this relationship as being physical and emotional; we do not realize that it is also etheric, and that the etheric factor is an exceedingly important one, and explains many things which cannot be explained in any other way.

Those who observe men and women know that if a group of women, however large, be cut off entirely from all association with males, a very peculiar mental atmosphere grows up among them, and they deteriorate individually, developing all manner of neurotic traits. This degeneration does not take place in the case of men; in fact, they tend periodically to seek seclusion from the society of women in order that they may, as it were, " be themselves " without restraint. It is also noticeable that in a group of women, even though they include no married women, if they either work with, or have social relations with men, the peculiar atmosphere and neurotic condition does not develop. What is the reason for this?

The reason is that the female receives etheric magnetism from the male whenever there is any degree of sympathy between them, whether in the comradeship of the workshop or the social relationships of dancing and dining or playing games together. The amount of magnetism she receives is in proportion to the degree of sympathy, which ranges from simple kindliness and good will, through all degrees of flirtation and love-making, up to the final consummation in physical union. Just as with vitamins, if this magnetism is completely lacking, deficiency diseases develop in course of time, but it only requires a very small proportion of this essential magnetism to maintain the soul in health. Enough can be picked up from even casual comradeships, provided there are plenty of them.

The male, for his part, is throwing off this magnetism all the time; therefore isolation from the companionship of women does not present a problem to him; on the other hand, if he is constantly in the company of women who are taking this magnetism from him, especially if he be the only male in a group of females, more magnetism tends to be drawn from him than he can comfortably spare, and his instinct is to seek comradeship in exclusively male society for a period, so that he has the use of his own magnetism for his own purposes, and can build up his personality without interference. The man who is constantly in the society of a group of women and lacks male companionship tends to lose his personality and be made negative; as witness the only son in a family of sisters where there is no father.

It has often been pointed out that there is a curious discrepancy in the relationship of the sexes, in that although the male has a definite physical need of the female, the female has no such need of the male. But this discrepancy is more apparent than real; for the female has just as definite an etheric need of the male as he has a physical need of her. It is this fact that holds incompatible couples together in the most surprising manner. One would think that their relationship would be a cause of nothing except mutual discomfort, and that they would be far happier apart; but as a matter of fact they have a curious need of each other, and are not content when separate.

This tie remains and binds, even when there has been legal divorce, until such time as both parties have formed fresh relationships. It is curious how much profound sex psychology was embodied in the old divorce law of England, which had grown up, like the rest of the common law, out of precedent and experience. That law declared that if adultery were condoned, that is to say, if the guilty party were received back into the marriage relationship again, there could be no divorce in respect of that offence. This is sound esoteric psychology; for the re-establishment of marriage relationship would renew the magnetic link, broken by the adultery.

In a happy marriage, where there is both affection and natural physical relationship—and no marriage can be happy without these two factors—a body of magnetism gradually builds up which includes both personalities in a single aura. It is in this single, shared aura that the real significance of marriage lies, as distinguished from irregular relationships. It is noteworthy that when pension inquiries during the War revealed how great was the number of unlegalized unions that were functioning as marriages, it became necessary to adjust the pension regulations accordingly, and the woman who had been regularly living with a man as his wife was enabled to draw separation allowance and pension in the event of his death. These unlegalized unions held for better for worse with exactly the same qualities of endurance as those that were recognized by Church and State.

It is this double aura which really constitutes the home. A married couple can make their home in a single room, and it can still be a home; they can make it in a caravan that moves on every day; they cannot make it, however, where there is no continuity of abiding-place, for the magnetism includes the objects in daily use. This is indicated in the popular expression, " Get a home together," which means obtain the needful furnishings for the carrying on of daily life.

Life inside this aura is entirely different to life outside it; for it has a peculiar power to inhibit outside influences. The person safe inside a well-established marriage aura is very resistive to suggestion coming from outside. This aura has a peculiar power to re-establish the poise of either partner when it has been shaken by the rubs of life; where there is mutual affection and respect, the self-esteem, shaken by the rude contacts of the world, is quickly restored. This is one of the most valuable things in marriage, for there is nothing more difficult than to handle affairs successfully when one's self-confidence is shaken.

This power of the home to resist outside interference is one of the last things to go when a marriage is breaking up. Anyone who has ever interfered between husband and wife does not need to be told this twice. They will stop any quarrel to unite against outside aggression.

When the marriage aura becomes well established the two are indeed made one, and each feels the other to be an extension of his or her self, so that any injury or depreciation to the one is felt as an injury to the other. Curiously enough, this applies even when there is ill will between the partners. Once the marriage aura has been established, it will stand a surprising amount of strain without giving way; it is this factor that complicates the divorce problem in a very curious manner. Unless there has been adultery, it is very difficult to dissolve a marriage aura. The act of adultery takes the guilty party right out of the marriage aura, and if he does not re-enter it by returning to eat and sleep under the family roof, he remains out, and the marriage ceases to function. Here again the common law speaks esoteric truth when it divorces "from bed and board." For it is a curious fact that to eat with a person establishes a psychic link. This is recognized in the customs of primitive peoples in relation to hospitality, especially among those who look upon hospitality as a sacred duty; the man with whom they have eaten is safe from attack for several hours after he leaves their camp, that is to say, until the food within him is digested. When a married couple reach the point when they take their meals separately, as well as occupy separate rooms, there is very little left of the marriage aura. The magnetism of the common meal is very potent; when a quarrel is made up, it is a common custom to have a drink together. When the point is reached where one person says to another, "I will not eat with you," the breach is unhealable. A very curious effect is produced by the person who refuses to share in a toast.

The evil effect of promiscuous relationships has its roots

in the damage it does to the etheric magnetism of both parties. No marriage aura can build up; consequently the peculiar steadying and protective effects of marriage are lacking; irregular relationships are a stimulant, but not a food; they create appetite, and never wholly satisfy it. For the significance of sex lies only partly on the physical plane; and where the relationship is limited to the physical, certain essential spiritual vitamins are still lacking. A marriage aura is a thing that takes time to establish. That is why newly married couples always go through a period of instability. It may look to them as if marriage were not serving its purpose; but that is only because the marriage is not yet established. It takes more than a signature in a register to make a marriage. Normally, when the marriage is a love-match, the first emotional rush carries them over this tentative period, and by the time the emotions are cooling down to normal, the development of the aura is well under way, and the first quarrels end in reconciliation, not separation, because the partners to the marriage discover that they have an indefinable need of each other.

It is this fact that makes bereavement a shock, even when the marriage has been nominally unhappy and full of friction. People may laugh at the grief of widows and widowers who were notorious for doing nothing but fight with their respective spouses; but nevertheless the sense of loss may be perfectly genuine. There is an old saying that all dead husbands are good husbands; and another to the effect that a bad husband is better than no husband at all. This indicates that a woman depends upon the magnetism of her mate to a far greater extent than is realized, and that she suffers serious loss when that magnetism is withdrawn.

A male, on the other hand, is naturally a polygamous creature; he does not depend on woman's magnetism in the same way; his dependance upon marriage, as distinguished from promiscuous relations, which meet his physical need well enough, is social, in its broadest and also in its highest sense where it merges into the spiritual. He needs his home as a place of refuge from the world; and this only the marriage aura can give him. But he also needs to escape from his home at regular and frequent intervals, lest his magnetism be drawn upon unduly and the integrity of his personality impaired.

CHAPTER XII

THE PROBLEM OF THE UNPOLARIZED

HAVING pointed out the importance of the exchange of magnetism between the sexes, I shall naturally be asked concerning the problem of the unmated, and therefore unpolarized. I have dealt with the psychological and physiological aspects of this problem in detail, together with their practical applications, in my book, *The Problem of Purity* (Rider), and there is therefore no occasion neither is this the place, to go into these aspects in their practical details. It may be of interest, however, to show the principles which must be taken into account in seeking a solution of this problem.

We live in an epoch of rapid changes in public opinion, and therefore in private conscience. The conditions that prevailed at the time *The Problem of Purity* was written have largely passed away. And although its practical advice is still valid, some of the problems it was designed to overcome have solved themselves. There is no longer the rigid taboo upon the discussion, or even the private study, of what the Americans call sexology. It would be difficult to find anyone nowadays who is fundamentally ignorant of the facts of life; nor, outside the ranks of the neurotic, will one find anyone who shies away from the subject in horror. It has taken its place along with such problems as sanitation and eugenics; it is one of the topics that are not usually broached at the dinner-table among those who have only just been introduced, but which can be dealt with without panic when the occasion arises. Our attitude towards sex is no longer comparable to the attitude towards ghosts of the person who has occasion to pass through the churchyard at midnight.

Experience shows that the average, healthy person of sound stock, who has had a reasonably wholesome upbringing, and is neither repressed nor stimulated in matters of sex, may have a certain amount of difficulty at the two periods of stress, puberty and the change of life, when the endocrines are temporarily out of balance, but that apart from this their physical sex-life is a self-regulating mechanism. If it is not, it is a case for the doctor, and probably quite a simple one. Much that in the old days was taken to a priest can be readily and effectually dealt with by an aperient.

The problem of non-polarization is not one that either arises or is solved on the physical plane alone. It occurs in marriage as well as out of it; and in fact, marriage breaks up on this point more often than on any other; nor is it only the childless marriages that split on this rock.

As seen in previous pages, the etheric magnetism radiated by the male is not limited in its manifestation to actual physical relations. It is concentrated there, it is true, but it is also being radiated all the time at a low potency. If therefore the unmarried woman has opportunity of comradeship and social intercourse with congenial males, she will get quite enough male magnetism to prevent her from suffering from a deficiency pathology analogous to those which occur when there is a lack of fresh fruit and green vegetables. The warping of character and conduct in the unpolarized female is just as much a deficiency disease as scurvy.

There is another factor, however, which plays a part in producing the symptoms of that condition which starts as prudery and, carried to extremes, becomes old maid's insanity. There are only three ways in which a woman can achieve independence and, consequently, the full development of her adult individuality. She must have private means; she must have adequate wage-earning capacity; or she must marry. Many pathologies which are regarded by the psycho-analysts as sex repressions are really individuality repressions, where some woman, dependent upon the whims of relatives for the means of existence, has been condemned to a narrow and thwarting life as the daughter at home. It is rare to see this type of pathology among bachelor women, even if the home of their bachelorhood be only a bed-sitting-room. Be it ever so humble, and be their means never so narrow, they can at least be themselves, and their personalities are not repressed or warped. There is all the difference in the world between a thwarting by circumstances from without, and the thwarting of impulses from within by a misplaced sense of duty, or lack of courage to do the thing that is desired.

We must remember, however, that there is just as wide a range in the needs of individuals with regard to their sex nature as there is in their appetite for food. There are persons for whom celibacy is unsatisfactory, or even incompatible with health and peace of mind. There are others who not only have no need of marriage, but would never make satisfactory mates. Both these extremes are within the limits of normality, happiness, and good morals provided square pegs are not driven ruthlessly into round holes. If one of the first type marries one of the second type, naturally there is trouble, though both might have been perfectly satisfactory mates for persons of their own type.

It is time we gave up thinking of sex as a vice, as the Christian thinks of it; or as a virtue, as the Hindu thinks of it, and regard it as a function. For that is how Nature thinks of it, and at the last resort she enforces her views. It is a function, however, which has to be exercised in relation to the rights and needs of other persons; it can never be an end in itself save for the heartless libertine. It is this social aspect of the sex problem that complicates it so much, and prevents it from being a simple problem of function, like nutrition. We shall get some salutary light on the problem, however, if we remember that there was a time when the amount a man drank was the subject of almost as rigorous social taboo as the purity of a woman is subject to nowadays. The teetotaller in a regimental mess in the good old days had just as bad a time of it as the unfortunate female who has lost her virtue. This should give us to think, and humble our spiritual pride.

Generation by generation, public opinion is coming more and more into line with physiological fact in relation to matters of sexual morality; and slowly but surely the law is catching up with public opinion. The more desperate problems of marriage and celibacy are becoming rarer. A marriage that has proved to be a mistake can be dissolved without ruining the lives of either party, provided the financial aspect is capable of solution. It is the throwing of a penniless, middle-aged gentlewoman upon the unskilled labour-market that is the real divorce problem. As far as social hardship or moral problems go, a man might keep as many ex-homes going as he could afford. That, in fact, is what high society does, and no one appears to be any the worse for it.

The acutest sex problems do not occur at the top of the tree, where there is sufficient money to allow of the free play of both temperaments; nor at the bottom, where the woman has to do her own housework and raise her children unaided; but in between, where there is neither enough money for freedom nor enough work for idle hands to do, and folk have time to get into mischief and to feel sorry for themselves.

The Society of the Inner Light, founded by Dion Fortune, has courses for those who wish seriously to pursue the study of the Western Esoteric Tradition; there is also a comprehensive Library. Enquiries should be addressed to:—

THE SECRETARY,
THE SOCIETY OF THE INNER LIGHT,
38, STEELE'S ROAD,
LONDON, N.W.3.